D0497337

Clive Gifford

Published in 2013 by Wayland

Copyright © Wayland 2013

Wayland
338 Euston Road
London NW1 3BH

Wayland Australia
Level 17/207 Kent Street
Sydney NSW 2000

Editor: Julia Adams
Designer: Jason Anscomb (www.rawshock.co.uk)
Picture Researcher: Diana Morris
Consultant: Dr Andrew Dilley
Proof reader and indexer: Sarah Doughty

British Library Cataloguing in Publication Data
Gifford, Clive.
    The who's who of World War I.
    1. World War, 1914-1918--Biography--Juvenile
literature.
    I. Title II. World War I
    940.4'00922-dc22
ISBN 978 0 7502 7950 5

Picture acknowledgements:
Australian War Memorial Negative Number
H15655: 13. Cody Images; 15, 16. 20, 21,
24. Corbis: front cover. A.R. Coster/Topical
Press/Getty Images: 9. The Granger Collection
NYC/Topfoto: 7, 22, 23, 26, 27, 28t, 28b, 29.
Hulton Archive/Getty Images: 19. Picturepoint/
Topham: 5, 17, 18. Topfoto: 4, 6, 12. Ullstein/
AKG Images: 10. Ullsteinbild/Topfoto: 14, 25.
Ken Welsh/Topfoto: 11. World History Archive/
Topfoto: 8.

Printed in China

10 9 8 7 6 5 4 3 2 1

Wayland is a division of Hachette Children's
Books, an Hachette UK company.

www.hachette.co.uk

Disclaimer:
The website addresses (URLs) included in this
book were valid at the time of going to press.
However, because of the nature of the Internet, it
is possible that some addresses may have changed,
or sites may have changed or closed down since
publication. While the author and Publisher
regret any inconvenience this may cause the
readers, no responsibility for any such changes can
be accepted by either the author or the Publisher.

Contents

World War I

World War I began in August 1914 and ended on 11 November 1918 when an agreement to stop fighting, called the Armistice, was signed. The war was mainly fought in Europe and the Middle East. It is known as the first 'world war' because soldiers from all over the globe took part and its effects were felt over many parts of the world.

In the years leading up to 1914, there were increasing tensions and rivalries between the great powers of Europe. Arms races were taking place between rival countries, some of whom had fought smaller wars in the past, winning or losing colonies around the world. In other parts of Europe, peoples sought independence from the giant empires that controlled them. Complicated alliances between different countries also made the situation unstable. It only took a single event to trigger major conflict. This occurred on 28 June 1914 with the assassination of Archduke Franz Ferdinand, the heir to the throne of Austria (see page 6).

German troops prepare to leave their trenches and go 'over the top' to fight. Over two million German soldiers died during World War I.

In a complex series of events and alliances, the two sides of the conflict lined up. The central powers were made up of Germany, Austria-Hungary and the Turkish Ottoman Empire with their allies. Against them were the Allied powers, which consisted of many countries including France, Russia, Britain and their empires. From 1917, the United States joined the Allied forces.

World War I lead to the end of four empires – Austria-Hungary, the Ottoman Empire, Germany and Russia.

In Russia, communism took over from a dynasty of Tsar rulers. At the time, World War I was known as 'The War To End All Wars'. However, many historians believe that the conflict and the peace agreements made afterwards created the conditions that helped lead to World War II.

The Treaty of Versailles was signed in June 1919. Germany fared badly under the peace agreement, losing around one-eighth of its territory. It also had to give up most of its military force and was ordered to pay huge amounts of reparations – sums of money or goods as war damages – to other nations.

Loss of life

Many leaders of the major European powers in World War I expected a quick victory. The opposite proved the case. Much of the conflict was carried out in horrific trench warfare. Especially on the Western Front, every kilometre of territory was won slowly and with an enormous loss of human life. New technologies, including machine guns, more powerful bombs and cannon shells, aircraft, tanks and poisonous gas, all took their toll. About 65 million soldiers from over twenty-five countries took part in the war. Over 9.7 million died and a further 21 million were wounded. Civilians suffered badly as well with over 8.8 million deaths. This was the greatest loss of life through combat the world had ever seen.

Gavrilo Princip

Born in the village of Obljaj, Gavrilo Princip was brought up in Bosnian's Serbian community when it was part of the Austria-Hungary empire. Only two of his eight brothers and sisters reached adulthood and Princip suffered ill health throughout his short life. As a student, he became involved with the movement *Mlada Bosna* (Young Bosnia), which demonstrated in 1912 for independence from Austria-Hungary.

BORN: 13.07.1894

NATIONALITY: Bosnian Serbian

PROFESSION: Member of the Black Hand

DIED: 28.04.1918

The situation in the Balkans (south-eastern Europe) had been unstable for many years. In 1912-13, two short but bloody wars had allowed Serbia and its allies, Greece, Montenegro and Bulgaria, to capture territory from Austria-Hungary. Tensions remained high, and as a member of Young Bosnia, Princip came to the attention of a secret group in Serbia known as the Black Hand. In June 1914, the heir to the throne of Austria-Hungary, Archduke Franz Ferdinand, announced a visit to Sarajevo in Bosnia. The Black Hand sent assassins to strike, one of whom was Princip.

The first attempt on the Archduke's life in Sarajevo was unsuccessful. A grenade was thrown, but it exploded behind his car, where it injured the other passengers, but not the Archduke. As a result, the Archduke's travel plans were changed that day. Princip gave up and was in Franz Joseph Street to eat a meal when the Archduke's car turned down the same road. Princip seized his chance. He fired two bullets from less than two metres away, killing Franz Ferdinand and his wife, Sophie.

Colonel Dragutin Dimitrijević led the Black Hand group, which recruited Princip to carry out the assassination. Dimitrijević was arrested and executed in 1917 by the Serbian government.

Princip had been ordered to commit suicide after the assassination. The 19-year-old turned his gun on himself, but it was wrestled from his hand and he was arrested and charged.

Under Austria-Hungarian law, citizens had to be twenty years or over to receive the death penalty. Princip was twenty-seven days too young, so he received the maximum prison sentence of twenty years instead. While the war waged in his home country and throughout Europe, Princip became the forgotten man of the conflict. He remained imprisoned throughout the war, suffering an amputation of the arm caused by bone tuberculosis. He was poorly fed and weighed only 40 kg at the time of his death.

Chain reaction

Events moved rapidly after the death of Franz Ferdinand. Austria-Hungary declared war on Serbia on 28 July 1914. Russia supported Serbia, while France had an alliance with Russia. The Germans, who had promised support to Austria-Hungary in advance, had developed war plans. These plans were based on a quick, surprise attack on France. Germany declared war on Russia on August 1 and on France two days later. As the German forces advanced, they invaded Belgium. Britain had an agreement to protect Belgium and entered the war on 4 August 1914.

Princip is arrested by Austro-Hungarian police shortly after assassinating the Archduke and his wife.

Edith Cavell

Before training as a nurse in London, Edith Cavell worked in Belgium, looking after a family's children. In 1907 she was appointed matron of *L'École d'Infirmière Dimplonier* – Belgium's first training school for nurses. Cavell earned a reputation as a highly skilled nurse and teacher who was strict but fair with junior nurses and trainees.

BORN: 04.12.1865

NATIONALITY: English

PROFESSION: Nurse

DIED: 12.10.1915

Cavell helped train dozens of new nurses before the hospital was taken over by the Red Cross at the start of the war. The German armies advanced into Belgium quickly and had occupied Brussels by the end of August 1914. Cavell insisted on treating all wounded people, no matter which side they fought on. In November 1914, two British soldiers trying to escape from the Germans asked for her help. She hid them for two weeks until a guide took them over the border into the Netherlands, where they were safe.

News of Cavell's actions reached an underground group trying to help escapees. She was contacted and agreed to help, housing Allied soldiers in secret in the Institute and helping to arrange food, money and identity papers for the men. This work, carried out in German-occupied Brussels, was extremely dangerous. Sudden police visits and searches were always a threat.

Cavell (above) became one of the best-known of the British women killed during World War I. Her story was made into a 1939 film starring actress Anna Neagle.

Propaganda purposes

Governments on all sides invented or twisted stories and information to boost their cause, something often described as propaganda. The British used Edith Cavell's death as a propaganda weapon against the Germans. They released the story in the United States to get the public there to turn against Germany. The British also used propaganda at home to strengthen the public's will to fight the Germans. Posters and postcards and written accounts of her death showed her as an innocent young woman. She was, in fact, forty-nine years old and had helped over 200 enemy soldiers to escape.

Cavell worked normally during the day as a nurse and then helped soldiers to escape, mainly at night. The number of British, French and Belgian troops Cavell housed and helped escape is probably over 200.

The Germans became suspicious and put Cavell's workplace under surveillance. She was warned that the Germans were closing in and that she should escape, but she refused, insisting on doing her duty. In August 1915, she was arrested by the Germans, held in prison for 10 weeks and then sentenced to death. Diplomats from both Spain and the United States tried to get her sentence reduced to imprisonment, but to no avail. Cavell was shot by a firing squad at the national rifle range in Brussels at 2 am in the morning on 12 October 1915. She was temporarily buried next to the prison where she had been held.

In May 1919, Cavell's body was returned to England. A funeral procession through London was attended by large crowds before her body was taken to be reburied in Norwich Cathedral.

Walther Schwieger

BORN: 07.04.1885

NATIONALITY: German

PROFESSION: U-Boat Commander
(Kapitänleutnant)

DIED: 05.09.1917

Born into a noble German family, Schwieger joined the German navy in 1903. He moved from serving on torpedo boats to sailing on larger ships. In 1911 he was transferred to the *U-boot Waffe* – the submarine arm of the German navy. Germany entered World War I with more than thirty-five U-boats (from the German word *Unterseeboot*, meaning undersea boat). In December 1914, Schwieger became captain on one of them.

Schwieger was a popular commander and proved a ruthless underwater hunter in the U-20, the U-boat he was captaining. His 64 m-long submarine could travel many thousands of kilometres on patrols above water, but much shorter distances underwater. It was armed with a deck-mounted gun and six torpedoes per journey. The U-20 sank more than thirty-five ships, mainly cargo ships carrying supplies to Britain.

Schwieger and the U-20's most famous victim was the giant passenger liner, RMS *Lusitania*, on 7 May 1915. The *Lusitania* was returning from New York to Liverpool with almost 2,000 people on board. The Germans had warned that they might attempt to sink it, and Schwieger fired a single torpedo. The explosion of the direct hit was followed by a second, bigger explosion. This may have been the ship's boilers, or the cargo of ammunition the Germans believed was onboard.

Schwieger was intent on heading back to base the day that the *Lusitania* was spied and sunk. His submarine had only three torpedoes left and was relatively low on fuel.

The 240 m-long RMS *Lusitania* took just eighteen minutes to sink following a torpedo hit by the U-20 – the submarine that Schwieger commanded.

The *Lusitania* sank, killing 1,198 passengers. Of those killed, 128 were Americans. This caused outrage in the US.

When the U-20 ran aground off the coast of Denmark in November 1916, the Germans destroyed it to stop it falling into British hands. Schwieger took command of a new submarine, the U-88, and continued to patrol and sink enemy ships. In four patrols in 1917, the U-88 sank twelve ships and damaged two more. But, on 5 September 1917, the U-88 hit a British mine in the North Sea and sank. All forty-three onboard, including Schwieger, died. British newspapers had called Schwieger 'the Baby Killer' after he sank the *Lusitania*. But after his death he was awarded Germany's highest honour, the *Pour Le Merite* medal, also known as the Blue Max.

Submarine warfare

The German U-boats waged war on merchant (non-military) ships travelling in the Atlantic and North Sea. Germany's plan was to stop food, supplies and weapons reaching Britain and France. The aim was to damage those countries' economies so that they had to surrender. At the start of 1915, the Germans stepped up their U-boat attacks and waged unrestricted submarine warfare (USW). This meant attacking any target and giving no warning. They stopped this practice after the sinking of the *Lusitania*, because they feared the United States might enter the war. In 1917, shortly after Germany had restarted USW, the United States did enter the war. In total, Germany's U-boat force sank over 5,000 ships, proving without doubt that submarines were a deadly weapon.

Albert Jacka

When World War I began, Albert Jacka was working as a forester in the Australian state of Victoria. Like many thousands of Australian and New Zealand men, he volunteered for service. ANZAC (Australian and New Zealand Army Corps) troops fought alongside the British throughout the rest of the war. Jacka's unit was sent first to Cairo, in Egypt, where the soldiers had ten weeks of training. In April 1915, Jacka was sent to the front as part of the large force that was to invade Gallipoli in Turkey (see panel, right).

BORN: 10.01.1893

NATIONALITY: Australian

PROFESSION: Infantryman

DIED: 17.01.1932

Fighting on Gallipoli was fierce, with both side's trenches and positions often extremely close to each other. Jacka's trench was invaded by Turkish soldiers on 19 May 1915. He fought furiously, as well as dragging wounded colleagues to safety.

When night came, he launched a one-man attack to re-take his unit's trench and succeeded against the odds. For these acts of bravery, Jacka became the first Australian to win the Victoria Cross, the highest decoration for valour that can be given.

ANZAC infantry surge ashore after landing on the coast of Gallipoli. This campaign resulted in a heavy toll on ANZAC forces, 11,400 of whom lost their lives.

Transferred to Western Europe, Jacka led from the front in a number of daring raids and attacks. He was a fearless fighter and was wounded three times at Pozières, France, in August 1916, but still managed to stop German troops advancing. At Bullecourt in April 1917, he captured two German soldiers, even though his gun was broken. Despite suffering injuries, including being shot by a sniper, Jacka was promoted to captain.

He was highly respected by the men under his command, but also not afraid to criticise the officers who ranked above him. This may be why his heroism did not earn him a higher promotion or a second Victoria Cross.

In May 1918, Jacka suffered more injuries in combat. He was wounded in the throat and became the victim of a German poisonous gas attack. He was transported back to England where doctors fought hard to save his life. He survived, and as a result Jacka was one of the very last Commonwealth soldiers to return home in 1919. He received a heroes' welcome in the city of Melbourne.

Albert Jacka proudly wearing his uniform and his medals, which included the Victoria Cross, the Military Cross and bar (meaning awarded twice). After returning to Australia, Jacka ran a business and was elected Mayor of St Kilda.

The 1915 Gallipoli Campaign

Britain was keen to knock the Ottoman Empire out of the war, leaving Germany without one of its major allies. The British war secretary General Kitchener, and the head of the navy Winston Churchill, planned a major invasion. British, French and ANZAC troops were to invade the Gallipoli peninsular and march on Constantinople (now Istanbul), the capital of the Ottoman Empire. The attack failed due to poor planning and leadership and fierce Turkish resistance. Around 47,000 French and half of the 410,000 British and ANZAC troops were killed or seriously wounded. The remainder were evacuated in the winter of 1915. The Turks had fought off the invasion, but lost a similar number of soldiers, weakening them in the later years of World War I.

Manfred von Richthofen

BORN: 02.05.1892

NATIONALITY: German

PROFESSION: Fighter pilot

DIED: 21.04.1918

In 1903, 11-year-old Manfred von Richthofen was enrolled at a military school. He became a cavalry officer in the German army. In May 1915 he transferred to the Imperial German Army Air Service, starting out as an observer in two-seater aircraft. In 1915, he applied for pilot training. Richthofen proved a natural, taking his first solo flight after just twenty-four hours of training.

In August 1916, Richthofen met German flying hero Oswald Boelcke, who was looking for talented pilots to form a new fighter plane squadron, Jasta 2. Richthofen was selected and scored his first 'kill' the following month. He was not a very daring fighter pilot. He was, however, an excellent marksman and cool and calculating under pressure. As he grew in experience, he learned to always seek an advantage before attacking. He often tried to attack with the sun behind him to blind the enemy.

Richthofen's number of kills mounted and made him famous. He received the Blue Max medal after he shot down sixteen enemy aircraft, and in January 1917 he was put in charge of his own squadron, Jasta 11. Within months, three other Jastas joined Jasta 11 to make one large unit called JG1. They were all under Richthofen's command. The unit became known as Richthofen's Flying Circus due to its colourful aircraft markings that were used as an identification aid in battle. In Germany, he was called the Red Battle Flier and in Britain his nickname was the Red Baron.

Manfred von Richthofen poses in front of a downed British fighter plane. His brother, Lothar, also became a fighter joining Jasta 11 in 1917 and shooting down more than forty enemy aircraft.

German aviators inspect a Fokker Dr. 1 triplane. Richthofen scored the last twenty of his kills flying this aircraft, which had a maximum speed of 185 km/h (115 mph) and was just 5.77 m (19 feet) long.

Richthofen was wounded in July 1917, but he returned to service later that year. He learned to fly a new aircraft – the small, highly agile three-winged fighter plane Fokker Dr. 1. Richthofen was impressed stating, 'they are manoeuvrable as the devil and climb like monkeys'. In his DR. 1, painted bright red, he shot down 80 enemy aircraft – the highest amount by any World War I fighter pilot. In April 1918, Richthofen was pursuing his eighty-first enemy target when Australian gunners on the ground and a pilot in an enemy fighter opened fire. A bullet damaged Richthofen's heart and lungs. He managed to land his aircraft safely, but died moments later.

Aircraft attack

At the start of World War I, aircraft design and construction was still in its early stages. Many of the planes were fragile and unreliable, and generals thought they were only useful for spotting enemy troops from the air. As the war progressed, aircraft design developed rapidly and military air forces became far more important. The invention of the interrupter gear in Germany in 1915 meant that, for the first time, aircraft could fire guns forward through their propeller blades. Dedicated fighter planes were developed. This made a war in the air possible, with fighters attacking enemy fighters, as well as attacking ground troops and shooting down enemy observation planes in the air.

Douglas Haig

Scotsman Douglas Haig became an officer in the British army in 1884. He was put in charge of a large section of the British Expeditionary Force at the start of the war, and by the end of 1914 he was promoted to General. A year later, he was made commander-in-Chief of the entire British force in Europe. Haig used tactics from the past, including cavalry charges and slow forward advances by infantry. He disliked or distrusted much of the new technology available and in 1915, said 'The machine gun is a much over-rated weapon.'

BORN: 19.06.1861

NATIONALITY: Scottish

PROFESSION: British Army General
Field Marshal

DIED: 29.01.1928

In the summer of 1916, Haig launched a big attack against German troops in the Somme region of France. It started with eight days of bombardment of the German lines by artillery. This was designed to damage the enemy, so that Allied troops could advance almost unopposed. The bombardment was unsuccessful and was one of a number of blunders. On the first day of their advance, 60,000 of Haig's forces were killed or wounded. But the attacks were continued for four months without any change in tactics. Haig commanded from his headquarters, about 80 km (50 miles) away from the fighting. At the end of the campaign, over one million soldiers were killed or wounded on both sides and the Allies only advanced a few kilometres. Despite criticism, Haig kept his command and was even promoted to Field Marshal in 1917.

During the war, Haig clashed with the Secretary of State for War, and later Prime Minister, David Lloyd George, over his tactics at the Somme.

Canadian troops go over the top during the Battle of the Somme in 1916.
Over 24,000 Canadian troops were killed or wounded during this campaign.

Haig's status as one of the most controversial figures of World War I was sealed with a new offensive that began in July 1917. Passchendaele (also known as the Third Battle of Ypres) resulted in a further half a million Allied troops killed, injured or captured for an Allied advance of just 8 km (5 miles). Haig was more successful near the end of the war.

Then the Allies achieved a dozen major victories from August to November 1918 as Germany was defeated. By this time, new technologies, such as tanks, and new tactics, such as dropping ammunition by aircraft, were being used. Haig retired from military service in 1921, the same year that he helped establish the British Legion for war veterans.

Butcher of the Somme

The Somme offensive lead to the death of a huge amount of soldiers. This gave rise to Haig's nickname 'Butcher of the Somme'. David Lloyd George, the War Minister and later Prime Minister, called the offensive, 'the most gigantic, tenacious, grim, futile and bloody fight ever waged in the history of war.' The morale dropped among Haig's soldiers and the British public, who were shocked at the number of deaths. Some historians argue that, while there were mistakes, Haig had little alternative and was trying to relieve the pressure on French forces at Verdun. Some also argue that this offensive seriously weakened Germany in future battles.

Flora Sandes

About 80,000 women were employed during World War I as nurses and orderlies at field hospitals. These were usually some distance away from the fighting. Only very few women entered active service in armies. Flora Sandes is one such example.

The daughter of a clergyman, Flora Sandes grew up in the small Yorkshire town of Poppleton. She became a nurse and worked for the St John Ambulance and later worked for the First Aid Nursing Yeomanry (FANY) in Britain.

BORN: 22. 01. 1876

NATIONALITY: English

PROFESSION: Nurse-turned-soldier in the Serbian Army

DIED: 1955 (exact date unknown)

Sergeant Major Flora Sandes wears her Serbian army uniform and medals to pose for a photo.

When World War I began, Sandes was thirty-eight. She volunteered immediately for an ambulance unit in Serbia that was run by the Red Cross. In 1915, the Serbian army retreated through the Albanian mountains from the armies of Austria-Hungary and Bulgaria. Sandes became separated from her unit and was caught up in battle with a unit of the Serbian Second Infantry Regiment. Picking up a weapon to defend herself, she impressed the company commander, Colonel Militch and became a soldier in the regiment.

Sandes was promoted to corporal and then sergeant. She could drive, ride a horse well, shoot and speak four languages. Fearless in battle, the male soldiers trusted her and she was promoted to lead a unit, often engaging in hand-to-hand fighting. In August 1916, the Serbian Army were advancing towards Monastir (now Bitola in Macedonia) when she was wounded by an enemy grenade. While she was recovering from her wounds, she was awarded Serbia's highest wartime medal, the Karageorge (the equivalent of Britain's Victoria Cross). Sandes returned to England, but Serbia was still in her mind. She raised money to help the Serbian people and wrote a book about her experiences called *An English Woman-Sergeant in the Serbian Army.*

American female nurses carry gas masks with them as they walk through trenches in France. More than 1,500 female nurses from the United States served in the forces during the world war.

As soon as she could, Sandes returned to Serbia. She remained in the Serbian Army after the war ended. In June 1919, a special Act of Parliament in Serbia was passed to make Sandes the first woman to be commissioned as an officer in the Serbian Army. When Flora Sandes retired with the rank of captain, she toured Britain, France, Canada and Australia, giving talks about her life.

At the age of sixty-four, Sandes returned to serve in the Serbian forces – this time in World War II. She was captured in uniform by the Germans and taken to a military prison hospital. She managed to escape wearing women's clothes that somebody had smuggled into prison for her. In the 1940s, Sandes left Serbia and returned to England where she lived until her death in 1955.

Women at war

Flora Sandes was one of a few women who fought openly alongside male soldiers. Many others disguised themselves as men. In 1914, Dorothy Lawrence managed to trick her way into serving in the British Expeditionary Force, but she lasted only ten days before being discovered. Russian Olga Krasilnikov was more successful. Disguised as a man, she fought in over fifteen battles in Poland and was awarded the Russian Cross of St. George medal. Another Russian, Maria Bochkareva, formed the first all-women's fighting unit in 1917. The First Russian Women's Battalion of Death contained around 300 female soldiers.

T.E. Lawrence

Fascinated by archaeology, Thomas Edward Lawrence had travelled through large parts of the Middle East and Turkey's Ottoman Empire before World War I. Lawrence was asked to help prepare British military maps of that region and was posted to Cairo during the early stage of the war. There he met many Arab leaders who wanted independence for their lands from the Ottoman Empire.

BORN: 15.08.1888

NATIONALITY: English

PROFESSION: Archaeologist, writer, military advisor (1939-45)

DIED: 19.05.1935

The Allied forces wanted to work with local Arabs to attack the Ottoman Empire. However, gaining their trust proved hard until Lawrence arrived. His love and deep knowledge of the people and customs of the region impressed a number of Arab leaders, and he became a military advisor to the powerful Arab leader, Emir Faisal. Lawrence dressed in the same way as his hosts, learned to ride a camel well and developed close friendships with many Arabs.

From the end of 1916 onwards, Arab units, often with Lawrence involved, made many hit and run attacks on Ottoman targets, particularly train lines. For the Allies to successfully attack the southern Ottoman Empire, they needed control of a port in the Red Sea which they could sail their own troops and supplies into. Aqaba, at the northern tip of the Red Sea, was chosen.

Lawrence used his local knowledge, bold plans and his ability to develop trust with local Arab leaders to mobilise Arab support and harass the Ottoman Empire forces effectively.

Lawrence and about 500 Arabs on camels took two months to cover a hazardous 800 km (497 mile) journey through enemy territory. In July 1917, they managed to capture Aqaba. The Arab forces pushed on and in October 1918 they entered the city of Damascus in Syria. Lawrence suffered a number of narrow escapes along the way, including having his camel shot from underneath him. In November 1917, he was captured by the Turks and beaten and tortured before he escaped.

After the war, Lawrence kept his close ties with the Arab people and campaigned for Arab independence from European control. Later, he joined the British tank corps under the name T.E. Shaw. He finally left the military in February 1935 and was killed in a motorcycle accident a few months later.

End of an empire

The British had captured Basra (in modern Iraq) in the early stages of the war, but the disastrous Gallipoli Campaign (see panel, page 13) held off a major invasion of the Ottoman Empire's territory. As the war progressed, the Allied powers began to capture key parts of the Ottoman Empire. Baghdad and Aqaba were captured in 1917, followed by Damascus, Jerusalem and the Ottoman capital, Constantinople (now Istanbul) in 1918. The Ottoman Empire signed the Armistice of Mudros on 30 October 1918. The Empire, which had lasted over 600 years, was broken up and its army disbanded.

Arab forces arrest thieves after they have captured the Syrian city of Damascus in 1918 from the Ottoman Empire armies.

Vladimir Lenin

Lenin was 16 when his father, a government official, died. A year later, his elder brother, Aleksandr, was executed for taking part in a bomb plot to assassinate the Russian Empire's ruler, Tsar Alexander III. Lenin began studying law and meeting revolutionaries. Over the next decade, he became a revolutionary leader and political thinker who was arrested by the Russian police and exiled to Siberia in 1897.

BORN: 24.04.1870

NATIONALITY: Russian

PROFESSION: Revolutionary leader

DIED: 24.01.1924

On his release from exile in 1900, Lenin lived mostly outside of Russia in various European cities. There, he raised funds and wrote pamphlets to build support. Lenin wanted to build a socialist state with the help of a revolution led by peasants in the country and the working classes in the towns.

When World War I began, Lenin was living in Austria and Switzerland. He continued to call for revolution. By late 1916, the Russian people had become tired of the war and their leaders, and strikes and protests grew and grew. In early 1917, a sudden revolution started in Petrograd. It led to the fall the Tsar, Nicholas II. A provisional government was put in place. With German help, Lenin arrived back in Russia at Petrograd (St Petersburg) in April 1917. The Germans hoped he could spread further disorder in Russia.

Lenin (centre) with his successor, Josef Stalin (left) and Mikhail Kalinin (right) at a meeting of the Russian Communist Party. Lenin felt that capitalism had made World War I inevitable. He pulled Russia out of the war as soon as an agreement with Germany could be reached.

The provisional government was re-organised a number of times, but unrest grew again. There were street uprisings in Petrograd in July 1917. In October, Lenin managed to convince many communists and supporters to seize power. He became the new leader of Russia in November, but faced many difficulties. He survived an assassination attempt at the start of 1918 and pulled Russia out of the war by signing a peace agreement with Germany (see panel, below). Differences with other political groups prompted Lenin and his supporters to split from them and rename themselves the Russian Communist Party in 1919. By that time, Russia was in the grip of a vicious civil war between Lenin's supporters and the White Army – a loose alliance of many different groups against communism or loyal to the Tsar. The war raged on for three years with both sides committing terrible war crimes. Lenin and the Russian Communist Party secured victory in 1921, but the country suffered greatly from the civil war. Lenin tried to develop communist

Lenin urges ordinary Russians to rise up and engage in a communist revolution in this painting by Irakli Toidze.

policies to help rebuild Russia and its economy. In 1922, he suffered a stroke. Two years later he died and Josef Stalin became the country's leader.

The Treaty of Brest-Litovsk

As soon as he came to power, Lenin argued for Russia to immediately cease fighting. A ceasefire was organised with Germany in December 1917. But while some of his advisors disagreed with the Germans' harsh terms, the Germans broke the ceasefire and advanced further. In March 1918, Russia withdrew from the war by signing the Treaty of Brest-Litovsk. Due to this treaty, Russia lost much of its western territory to Germany. This included Poland, Belarus, the Ukraine and what later became the Baltic states (Estonia, Lithuania and Latvia). It also lost Ardahan, Bat'umi and Kars to the Ottoman Empire. Russia recovered these territories after the armistice and became the Soviet Union in 1922.

Erich Ludendorff

As a young man, Erich Ludendorff entered military cadet school and qualified ahead of his peers. He was extremely hardworking and moved up the ranks of the German military. In the years before World War I, Ludendorff was involved in perfecting the Schlieffen Plan for the invasion of France (see panel, right).

BORN: 09.04.1865

NATIONALITY: German

PROFESSION: Military commander

DIED: 20.12.1937

Ludendorff was involved in negotiating the treaty of Brest-Litovsk with Russia (see panel, page 23). He hoped this would free up resources to the east for a decisive offensive on the western front.

Within three weeks of the start of World War I, Ludendorff had earned Germany's highest military medal, the *Pour le Mérite*, for commanding forces that captured the Belgian city of Liège. Within days of receiving the medal, he was moved from the western to the eastern front. The Russians were threatening to capture Prussia, and Ludendorff was made Chief-of-Staff of the German Eighth Army, second in command to Paul von Hindenburg. The pair engineered two spectacular military victories – at Tannenberg in 1914 and the Battle of Masurian Lakes in 1915, where 100,000 Russian troops were captured.

These victories brought Hindenburg great acclaim, and in 1916 he was made Chief of Staff of the entire German army. He took Ludendorff as his deputy. Kaiser Wilhelm II gradually lost his power as a ruler, because Ludendorff, von Hindenburg and a handful of senior German officers and industrialists made all the key decisions about the economy and the military. In 1917, Ludendorff's advice was followed to return to unrestricted submarine warfare (see panel, page 11). As a result, the US officially declared war on Germany on 6 April 1917. Large numbers of American troops began arriving in Europe by the end of 1917.

The Schlieffen Plan

At the start of the war, Germany's strategy was based on a plan originally formed by the former head of its army, Count Alfred von Schlieffen. The plan assumed that Russia would take six weeks or more to mobilise its armies, giving Germany six weeks to invade France, capture Paris, and remove the French from the war. As a result, around 90 per cent of all German forces were to be concentrated in the west, with most of them invading France through Belgium. The plan worked well at first, but resistance in Belgium and by the British Expeditionary Force was stronger than anticipated. Germany's supply lines were stretched and Russia began to send its armies into eastern parts of Germany quicker than expected. Forced to send reinforcements, including senior generals like Ludendorff, to the east, Germany was pushed into fighting the war on two fronts.

Faced with this, Ludendorff and Hindenburg launched Germany's final gamble in March 1918 – a huge offensive aiming to break through the western front. This Second Battle of the Somme resulted in a German advance of around 65 km (40 miles), the most territory captured on the western front since 1914. But Germany failed to achieve a decisive break through enemy lines. Ludendorff called for an armistice and offered to resign in October 1918. He changed his mind, only to be dismissed anyway. Ludendorff proved an able behind-the-scenes organiser of the German military forces but blamed a lack of support from some Germans for his country's failure in the war.

Ludendorff (right) pores over a military map with Kaiser Wilhelm II (centre) and Paul von Hindenburg (left). Ludendorff and von Hindenburg made most of the key military and political decisions in the last years of the war.

Woodrow Wilson

After studying law, Woodrow Wilson became a successful university professor, specialising in political science. He entered politics as a Democrat, and was elected governor of New Jersey in 1910. Two years later he became President of the United States of America.

BORN: 28.12.1856

NATIONALITY: American

PROFESSION: Democrat politician and US President

DIED: 03.02.1924

Wilson insisted that the United States stay neutral after war broke out. Most Americans did not believe their country should enter a huge and expensive war. They felt it was being fought a long way away. Wilson had studied recent history and knew the reasons for the war were complex. The United States continued to trade with countries from both sides even after the outrage caused by Germany sinking the *Lusitania* liner in 1915 (see page 10).

In 1916, Wilson won his second presidential election. His campaign had emphasised peace and promised not to enter the conflict. He tried to use America's influence to end the war, appealing to the fighting nations to begin talks. This failed to work and startling news arrived in early 1917. First, in February, the Germans restarted unrestricted submarine warfare (see page 11). Second, in March, the British had decoded a secret telegram from German foreign minister, Arthur Zimmermann. It had proposed a military alliance with Mexico in which Germany would help Mexico regain its former territories of Texas, New Mexico and Arizona.

Wilson negotiated hard with other allied leaders to secure lasting peace after the end of World War I.

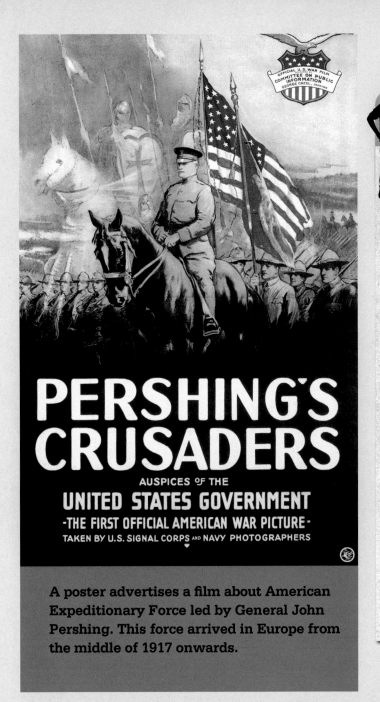

A poster advertises a film about American Expeditionary Force led by General John Pershing. This force arrived in Europe from the middle of 1917 onwards.

Segregated soldiers

Around 12 per cent of the American Expeditionary Force sent to World War I were African Americans. These men were usually segregated racially into black-only units led by white officers. Racism existed in the American army and many white commanders felt that their black soldiers were unsuitable for fighting. Most were employed as reserves or worked at ports and other places away from the fighting. Only a fifth of all black American soldiers saw action, many under the command of the French forces. One unit, the 369th Infantry Regiment, was at the front for six months, longer than any other. Nicknamed the Harlem Hellfighters, the regiment fought with great bravery and skill, and 171 of them were awarded the Legion of Merit medal.

Wilson eventually declared war on Germany and its allies on 6 April 1917, stating, 'the world must be made safe for democracy.' Within two months, the first of the 1.2 million-strong American Expeditionary Force arrived in Europe. This huge boost in reinforcements, along with American shipping and supplies, helped speed up the end of the war. Wilson was keen to develop a lasting peace, so he travelled to Europe after the end of the war to negotiate personally with European leaders. He wanted to prevent revenge on Germany and proposed an international body to solve future disputes. In 1919 this body became the League of Nations. Despite Wilson's involvement in its foundation, the US never joined the League. Wilson suffered a stroke in September 1919 but remained in office until 1921.

The War Poets

Many poems have been written in wartime, mostly celebrating a great victory or glorifying the battles fought. Much of the poetry of World War I was different. It was often written by young men and women who had served in the forces and saw war's devastation at first hand.

At the start of the war, some poetry was optimistic about a great victory. It was full of lines about serving one's country happily and with honour. Rupert Brooke, who died on a troop ship bound for Gallipoli in 1915, wrote, 'If I should die, think only this of me: / That there's some corner of a foreign field / That is forever England'.

Such poems contrast greatly with those written later in the war by men fighting at the front. Hundreds of servicemen chose to write poetry as a way of expressing their strong emotions about the waste of war and their shocking and terrifying experiences. Wilfred Owen wrote of, 'those who died as cattle' and, 'above all I am not concerned with poetry. My subject is war, and the pity of war.' Owen joined the British army in 1915. He was wounded in 1917, but returned to France where he was killed just one week before the end of the war. Winnifred Mary Letts wrote a poem called *The Deserter*. In it, she describes the feelings of a man scared by what he has experienced during the war. Not all World War I poems were against the war, but they often examined issues such as life and death, courage, duty and innocence.

While most attention is paid to the war poets who wrote in English, other nations also had poets who wrote about World War I. Hungarian Géza Gyóni's wartime poems began with hope and later became more sad and bitter. He died in a Russian prisoner camp in 1917. The German poet and playwright August Stramm's collection of wartime poems, *Dripping Blood*, was published after his death in 1915.

Fellow war poets Wilfred Owen (top) and Siegfried Sassoon (bottom) met when both were convalescing in Craiglockhart War Hospital in Edinburgh. Sassoon encouraged Owen to work on his poetry and pleaded with him not to go back to Europe to fight. Both men penned passionate poetry about the cost and suffering created by the war.

In Flanders Fields

John McCrae was a Canadian field doctor who served during World War I. His poem, *In Flanders Fields*, was written in May 1915, the day after he had witnessed the death of his friend, Alexis Helmer. McCrae was commander of a general hospital in Boulogne, France, when he died of pneumonia in 1918.

John McCrae had served in the artillery at the start of the war. *In Flanders Fields* was first published in December 1915 in the British magazine, *Punch*.

In Flanders Fields

In Flanders fields the poppies blow
Between the crosses, row on row
That mark our place; and in the sky
The larks, still bravely singing, fly
Scarce heard amid the guns below.

We are the Dead. Short days ago
We lived, felt dawn, saw sunset glow,
Loved and were loved, and now we lie
In Flanders fields.

Take up our quarrel with the foe:
To you from failing hands we throw
The torch; be yours to hold it high.
If ye break faith with us who die
We shall not sleep, though poppies grow
In Flanders fields.

Read It, See It, Hear It

Here are some website links to help you explore World War I poetry:

http://www.firstworldwar.com/poetsandprose/
A large collection of famous World War I poems.

http://www.bbc.co.uk/history/worldwars/wwone/wilfred_owen_gallery_01.shtml
See pictures of Wilfred Owen and hear audio retellings of some of his most famous poems.

http://www.ppu.org.uk/learn/poetry/poetry_ww1_1.html
Learn more about the background to John McCrae writing *In Flanders Fields*.

http://www.oucs.ox.ac.uk/ww1lit/education/online/siegfried-sassoon.html
A good collection of links to websites about the poet Siegfried Sassoon and other World War I poets.

Timeline: World War I

People	Events

People

Events

June 1914
Gavrilo Princip assassinates Archduke Ferdinand in Sarajevo. This murder triggers World War I

August 1914
Germany declares war on Russia and then France. Britain declares war on Germany.

May 1915
U-boat captain, Walther Schwieger sinks the giant liner, *Lusitania* in the Atlantic.

April 1915
Allied troops begin landings on the Gallipoli peninsula in Turkey.

October 1915
Edith Cavell executed for spying by German forces.

February-December 1916
Battle of Verdun – the longest battle of the war. Around one million die as a result.

July 1916
The Somme Offensive begins with Allied bombardment of German positions.

April 1917
US President Woodrow Wilson announces the United States is entering the war.

June 1917
First US troops arrive in Europe.

July 1917
Passchendaele (Third Battle of Ypres) is fought with heavy losses on both sides.

October 1917
Vladimir Lenin and the Russian Communist Party seize power in Russia.

March 1918
Russia signs the Treaty of Brest-Litovsk leaving the war fully and granting territory to the Central Powers.

April 1918
German flying ace Manfred von Richthofen is killed.

11 November 1918
Armistice signed between the Germans and the Allies.

January 1919
Peace conference begins in Paris leading to the Treaty of Versailles in June 1919.

Glossary

Allies the forces from Britain, France, from 1917, the USA, and other nations fighting Germany and its allies.

Brest-Litovsk, Treaty of an agreement between Russia and the Central Powers when Russia withdrew from the War.

Central Powers Germany, Austria-Hungary, Bulgaria and the Turkish Ottoman Empire.

communism a political system where the state controls property, production and trade.

Eastern Front name given to the fighting in eastern Europe.

League Of Nations a union of countries formed in 1919 by the Treaty of Versailles to build peace, security and promote settlements by negotiations not conflict.

mobilisation to make armed forces ready to move and fight.

morale the mood or confidence of a person, a military force or country's people.

no-man's land the barren territory that lay between the opposing Allied and German trenches on the Western Front.

offensive a major attack by one side's forces against another's.

peninsula narrow stretch of land that juts out into the sea.

propaganda spreading a particular message to try to influence public opinion or to make people perform certain actions.

reconnaissance scouting or spying to gain information about an enemy force's position, size and intentions.

torpedo a self-propelled missile fired from a ship, submarine or aircraft that explodes on impact.

trench warfare form of fighting whereby two sides fight each other from opposing trenches dug into the ground.

Western Front the name given to the stretch of land in France and Belgium between the North coast of Europe and the Swiss border where much of the fighting during World War I occurred.

Further information

Books To Read
Documenting History: World War I, Philip Steele, Wayland, 2009.

Wars Day By Day: World War 1, Jason Turner, Franklin Watts, 2008.

Presidents: Woodrow Wilson, Henry M. Holden, Enslow Publishers, 2003.

Famous Flyers: Manfred von Richthofen, Earle Rice, Chelsea House Publishers, 2003.

Lenin and the Russian Revolution, Steve Phillips, Heinemann, 2000.

Places To Visit
Imperial War Museum
Lambeth Road, London SE1 6HZ, England
Website: http://london.iwm.org.uk

The Passchendaele Museum
Ieperstraat 5, 8980 Zonnebeke, Belgium
Website: http://www.passchendaele.be

The Verdun Memorial Museum
1, Avenue du Corps Européen, 55100 Fleury-devant-Douaumont, France.
Website: www.memorial-de-verdun.fr

Websites
http://www.firstworldwar.com/bio/index.htm
A massive collection of short biographies of key people during World War I.

http://www.historylearningsite.co.uk/world_war_one.htm
Read detailed biographies of Erich Ludendorff, T.E. Lawrence and many others at this History Learning website.

http://www.worldwar1.com/
This huge website contains lots of fascinating features on World War I from over forty short biographies to photos and accounts of key battles.

http://www.bbc.co.uk/history/worldwars/wwone/index.shtml
The BBC's webpages contain the profiles of famous figures as well as descriptions of life in the trenches and key moments during the war.

http://www.pbs.org/greatwar/
A great website on World War I with videos, photos and quotes from key participants.

http://www.richthofen.com/
Read the complete autobiography online of Manfred von Richthofen published in 1917.

Index